The West

Arizona
California
Nevada

Kirsten W. Larson

Mason Crest
450 Parkway Drive, Suite D
Broomall, PA 19008
www.masoncrest.com

©2016 by Mason Crest, an imprint of National Highlights, Inc.

Printed and bound in the United States of America.

CPSIA Compliance Information: Batch #LES2015.
For further information, contact Mason Crest at 1-866-MCP-Book.

First printing
1 3 5 7 9 8 6 4 2

Library of Congress Cataloging-in-Publication Data

Larson, Kirsten W.
  The West : Arizona, California, Nevada / Kirsten W. Larson.
       pages cm. — (Let's explore the states)
  Includes bibliographical references and index.
  ISBN 978-1-4222-3337-5 (hc)
  ISBN 978-1-4222-8622-7 (ebook)
  1. Southwestern States—Juvenile literature. 2. Arizona—Juvenile literature.
  3. California—Juvenile literature. 4. Nevada—Juvenile literature. I. Title.
  F785.7.L37 2015
  979—dc23
                              2014050200

Let's Explore the States series ISBN: 978-1-4222-3319-1

Publisher's Note: Websites listed in this book were active at the time of publication. The publisher is not responsible for websites that have changed their address or discontinued operation since the date of publication. The publisher reviews and updates the websites each time the book is reprinted.

About the Author: As a child, Kirsten W. Larson lived near Phoenix. Today she writes from her home in California's Mojave Desert. She's written numerous articles, as well as many books for young readers, including *Using the Scientific Method* (Rourke, 2014).

Picture Credits: Featureflash: 40 (bottom); Intel, 20; Library of Congress: 13, 14, 15, 18 (lower left), 31, 32, 33, 34, 35 (top), 51; National Archives: 52, 53, 54; photo courtesy of National Nuclear Security Administration/Nevada Site Office: 55 (bottom); Richard M. Nixon Presidential Library and Museum: 40 (top left); courtesy Ronald Reagan Library: 40 (top right); used under license from Shutterstock, Inc.: 1, 5, 6, 11, 12, 18 (lower right), 22, 24, 27 (top right, bottom left), 37, 38 (right), 39, 41, 42 (bottom), 43, 49 (bottom), 50 (bottom), 55 (top); American Spirit/Shutterstock.com: 36 (top), 42 (top), 56, 57; Bildagentur Zoonar GmbH/Shutterstock.com: 9 (bottom left); Ser Borakovskyy/Shutterstock.com: 50 (top); S. Bukley/Shutterstock.com: 59; Creatista/Shutterstock.com: 17; Jeffrey M. Frank/Shutterstock.com: 9 (top left); Zack Frank/Shutterstock.com: 9 (top right), 28; Dan Holm/Shutterstock.com: 36 (bottom); Doug Meek/Shutterstock.com: 10; Nagel Photography/Shutterstock.com: 9 (bottom right); Aleksei Potov/Shutterstock.com: 27 (top left); Tim Roberts Photography/Shutterstock.com: 16, 19, 21; R. Gino Santa Maria/Shutterstock.com: 18 (top); Hank Shiffman/Shutterstock.com: 30; T Photography/Shutterstock.com: 44, 49 (top), 58; Richard Thornton/Shutterstock.com: 35 (bottom); Gary C. Tognoni/Shutterstock.com: 27 (bottom right), 38 (left); Andrew Zarivny/Shutterstock.com: 60.

Table of Contents

Arizona 7

    Arizona at a Glance, 6; Geography, 7; History, 10; Government, 17;
    The Economy, 19; The People, 20; Major Cities, 21; additional resources, 23.

California 25

    California at a Glance, 24; Geography, 25; History, 28; Government, 36;
    The Economy, 38; The People, 39; Major Cities, 42; additional resources, 45.

Nevada 47

    Nevada at a Glance, 46; Geography, 47; History, 48; Government, 56;
    The Economy, 57; The People, 59; Major Cities, 60; additional resources, 61–62.

Index 63

Series Glossary 64

KEY ICONS TO LOOK FOR:

Words to Understand: These words with their easy-to-understand definitions will increase the reader's understanding of the text, while building vocabulary skills.

Sidebars: This boxed material within the main text allows readers to build knowledge, gain insights, explore possibilities, and broaden their perspectives by weaving together additional information to provide realistic and holistic perspectives.

Research Projects: Readers are pointed toward areas of further inquiry connected to each chapter. Suggestions are provided for projects that encourage deeper research and analysis.

Text-Dependent Questions: These questions send the reader back to the text for more careful attention to the evidence presented there.

Series Glossary of Key Terms: This back-of-the book glossary contains terminology used throughout this series. Words found here increase the reader's ability to read and comprehend higher-level books and articles in this field.

LET'S EXPLORE THE STATES

Atlantic: North Carolina, Virginia, West Virginia

Central Mississippi River Basin: Arkansas, Iowa, Missouri

East South-Central States: Kentucky, Tennessee

Eastern Great Lakes: Indiana, Michigan, Ohio

Gulf States: Alabama, Louisiana, Mississippi

Lower Atlantic: Florida, Georgia, South Carolina

Lower Plains: Kansas, Nebraska

Mid-Atlantic: Delaware, District of Columbia, Maryland

Non-Continental: Alaska, Hawaii

Northern New England: Maine, New Hampshire, Vermont

Northeast: New Jersey, New York, Pennsylvania

Northwest: Idaho, Oregon, Washington

Rocky Mountain: Colorado, Utah, Wyoming

Southern New England: Connecticut, Massachusetts, Rhode Island

Southwest: New Mexico, Oklahoma, Texas

U.S. Territories and Possessions

Upper Plains: Montana, North Dakota, South Dakota

The West: Arizona, California, Nevada

Western Great Lakes: Illinois, Minnesota, Wisconsin

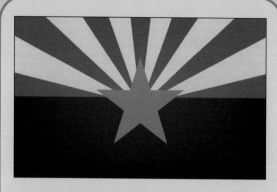

Arizona at a Glance

Area: 113,990 sq miles (295,233 sq km)[1]. 6th largest state
  Land: 113,594 sq mi (294,207 sq km)
  Water: 396 sq mi (1,026 sq km)
Highest elevation: Humphrey's Peak, 12,643 feet (3,854 m)
Lowest elevation: along Colorado River near Yuma, 70 feet (21 m)

Statehood: February 14, 1912 (48th state)
Capital: Phoenix

Population: 6,731,484 (15th largest state)[2]

State nickname: Grand Canyon State
State bird: cactus wren
State flower: saguaro cactus blossom

[1] U.S. Census Bureau
[2] U.S. Census Bureau, 2014 estimate

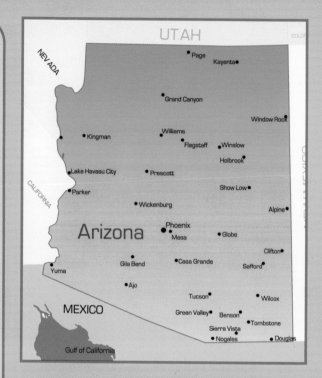

Arizona

Called the "Grand Canyon State," Arizona is home to far more than its striking landscape. The desert blooms with large cities like Phoenix, acres of farmland thanks to irrigation projects, and rich copper ore. No wonder its motto is *Ditat Deus*, or "God enriches."

Geography

Covering 113,990 square miles (295,233 square kilometers), Arizona is the sixth-largest state in the United States.

The Colorado River comprises most of Arizona's western border with California and Nevada. To the south lies Mexico. Utah borders Arizona to the north, while New Mexico lies to the east. Utah, New Mexico, Colorado, and Arizona come together in a place known as "Four Corners." The area is the only spot in the U.S. where four states touch.

The Colorado *Plateau* covers the northern part of the state. *Arroyos*, *buttes*, *canyons*, and *mesas* dot the landscape. About six million years ago, the Colorado River began to carve the most well-known feature in this area, the Grand Canyon. It stretches

277 miles (446 km) long, 18 miles (29 km) wide, and measures a mile (1.6 km) to the canyon floor.

The Colorado Plateau also is home to the Painted Desert, Petrified Forest, and the state's highest mountain, Humphrey's Peak, at 12,643 feet (3,854 m). The mountain is a former volcano located near Flagstaff.

The center of the state includes mountains and low-lying basins, many rich with copper. To the southwest is the Sonoran Desert.

Despite its *arid* climate, several rivers flow through Arizona. The Gila River and its tributaries drain more than half the state. Near Yuma, where the Gila meets the Colorado, sits the lowest point in the state, about 70 feet (21 m) above sea level. Up north, the Colorado River and Little Colorado River cross the state. Arizona has few

 # Words to Understand in This Chapter

arid—a dry climate.

arroyo—a dry creek that fills with water when it rains.

butte—a flat-topped hill or mountain that is taller than it is wide.

canyon—steep valley carved by a river.

deposits—layers of minerals.

immigration—moving from one country to another.

Jesuit—a member of a Roman Catholic order, the Society of Jesus.

mesa—a flat-toped hill or mountain that is wider than it is tall.

meteorite—a space rock that falls to Earth.

plateau—an area of relatively level high ground.

semiconductor—a material that can conduct electricity under some circumstances, but not others. Semiconducting material is used to make electronic circuits.

Theodore Roosevelt Dam on the Salt River is 357 feet (109 m) high. The large Theodore Roosevelt Lake has formed behind the dam, and its water is used to produce electricity, as well for irrigation projects.

The Gila River flows for 649 miles (1,044 km) through New Mexico and Arizona, where it enters the Colorado River. Much of its water is diverted from the river channel for irrigation.

Petrified Forest National Park in northeastern Arizona covers about 146 square miles (380 sq km). The park is rich with fossils from the late Triassic period, about 225 million years ago.

Colorful scenery can be found in the Painted Desert, which is located near the "Four Corners" region where the states of Arizona, Colorado, New Mexico, and Utah meet.

Monument Valley is a scenic area on the Navajo reservation in Arizona. The tallest of the sandstone buttes rise 1,000 feet (300 m) above the valley floor.

natural lakes. A series of dams creates artificial lakes, like Lake Powell, Lake Mead, and Lake Havasu.

"Dry" is the word that most sums up Arizona's climate. The low-lying central and southern portions of the state receive about 7 inches (18 cm) of rain each year. In summer, temperatures there top 100° Fahrenheit (38° Celsius). Meanwhile, places like Flagstaff and the Grand Canyon see snow in the winter. Overnight temperatures in those areas dip below freezing.

History

The earliest record of ancient people in Arizona includes spearheads found among mammoth bones from 12,000 years ago.

Arizona Attractions

Grand Canyon National Park invites visitors to hike or ride mules to the canyon floor. There, travelers can whitewater raft on the Colorado River.

More than 50,000 years ago, a space rock streaked through the sky and smacked the Earth forming a hole more than two miles (3.2 km) across. Today, Barringer *Meteorite* Crater remains one of the best-preserved impact craters in the world.

More than 800 years ago, the Sinagua people carved a 20-room apartment-like complex into limestone cliffs. Preserved at Montezuma Castle National Monument, the area is visited by 350,000 people a year.

Phoenix's Heard Museum of American Indian Art and History is world-recognized for vast collection of Native American artifacts, along with its cultural festivals.

Visitors experience life in the Old West at the Goldfield Ghost Town near Apache Junction. They pan for gold, watch quick-draw gunslingers, visit the Goldfield Mine and more.

The jail at Goldfield Ghost Town.

Baringer Crater, near Winslow.

Montezuma Castle is an ancient cliff dwelling.

Several ancient Native American cultures developed in different parts of the state in the years before the Spanish arrived. The Hohokam settled near modern-day Phoenix as early as 2000 BCE. They built villages and dug sophisticated irrigation canals with sticks to grow corn, beans, squash, and cotton. Today, the Tohono O'odham are believed to be the descendants of the Hohokam.

The ancestral Pueblo people lived in the northeast near the Colorado Plateau. By about 500 CE, they farmed corn, beans, and squash. Between 750 and 1300 CE, the group built multi-roomed pueblos, resembling modern day apartments. The Pueblo were some of the first Native Americans the Spanish encountered in the area. The modern-day Pueblo and Hopi trace their origins to this group.

The early groups scattered in the 1400s. In the 1600s the ancestors of the Apache and Navajo people moved into Arizona from the Great Plains.

The lure of gold brought the first Europeans from Mexico to modern-day Arizona. In 1539, Father Marco de Niza explored the region with his servant. He claimed to have found one of the seven cities of gold, which had been reported to exist in Spanish legends. The next year, he guided Spanish explorer Francisco Vázquez de Coronado to the region. However, Coronado found only an Indian pueblo. He kept searching, a trip that led him as far as Kansas.

One of the first Spanish missions in Arizona was San Xavier del Bac, founded in 1692 by Father Eusebio Kino. It is located about 10 miles (16 km) south of downtown Tucson, on the Tohono O'odham reservation.

For much of the colonial period (1540–1821), few Spanish settled in Arizona. In the 1620s, Franciscans established an unsuccessful mission in Hopi territory. Almost 70 years later, Father Eusebio Kino founded a more successful *Jesuit* missions in Tohono O'odham country. Still, the 1700s were marked by periods of attempted settlement, revolts by Native Americans, and increasing Spanish military presence.

When Mexico became independent from Spain in 1821, Arizona, as well as the rest of the southwest, became part of that new country. Arizona later became U.S. territory as part of the Treaty of Guadalupe Hidalgo, which ended the U.S. War against Mexico 1848.

Originally, Arizona was part of the New Mexico Territory. Its southern border was the Gila River. In 1853, however, the U.S. bought 30,000 square miles (77,700 sq km) south of the river from Mexico.

Mining helped the area grown in importance. In 1854, Charles Poston, known as the "Father of Arizona,"

Charles Poston was a miner and politician who played a key role in the establishment of Arizona as a U.S. territory. He later held several important positions in the government of the Arizona Territory.

began mining silver in Tubac. Poston's mines produced $3,000 worth of silver a day (about $85,000 in today's dollars). In 1861 Poston personally traveled to Washington, D.C. to lobby President Lincoln to make Arizona a separate territory. Lincoln granted Arizona territorial status in 1863.

Mining and ranching increased tensions with Native Americans throughout the late 19th century. The newcomers mined and drove cattle on Native American lands. Military leaders attempted to subdue natives. Kit Carson led a small army against the Navajo in 1863. When the the Indians did not surrender, Carson's party killed the men, burned fields, and marched women and children to a

Kit Carson was a reluctant, though highly effective, Indian fighter. Using merciless tactics to rid the area of Native Americans, he helped to change the face of the Southwest.

reservation at Bosque Redondo, New Mexico, more than 400 miles (644 km) away. Wars with various Native Americans continued in Arizona until 1886. That year, the Apache leader Geronimo surrendered his small fighting force.

Fighting with Native Americans was not the only danger for many set-

The Apache leader Geronimo often fought against Mexican troops, but also clashed with Americans in the southwest.

tlers. The Arizona territory remained a largely lawless place, especially in the mining towns that sprang up almost overnight. Gunfights settled many disagreements, as happened during the gunfight at OK Corral in Tombstone during October 1881.

During the 1880s, the U.S. government laid two railroad lines through Arizona. By 1886, ranchers who before had only sold their cows in Arizona could now send them to markets outside the territory. Railroad cars also hauled copper. The territory boomed. In the 1870s, fewer than 10,000 people had lived in Arizona. By 1900, that number was more than 120,000.

Efforts to improve working conditions for many miners helped spur statehood. Labor organizers believed that conditions would not improve as long as Arizona remained a territory. In 1910, President Taft signed legislation allowing Arizona to begin the process of statehood. On February 14, 1912, Arizona officially became the 48th state.

World War I spurred growth of the

President William Howard Taft signs the bill that allows Arizona to enter the Union as the 48th state in 1912.

new state's economy. Tire manufacturers grew pima cotton near Phoenix. This cotton was used in the tires and fabrics for military airplanes.

After the Great Depression, World War II turned the state's fortunes around. In 1949, Motorola located its Military Electronics Division in Phoenix. Throughout the 1950s, many high tech companies came to the city. The invention of air conditioning helped fuel growth of these industries, keeping both electronics and people cool.

Arizona's weather attracted military bases to the region during this period. It also brought retirees. During the 1960s, Del Webb founded Sun City, a haven for active retirees.

 Did You Know?

Philip Johnston, a missionary who grew up on an Arizona Navajo reservation, suggested using the Navajo language for a code during World War II. Soon after the attack on Pearl Harbor, 29 Navajo joined the first class of "Navajo Code Talkers" and developed the unbreakable communication code.

The Arizona Canal flows past suburbs and golf courses in Scottsdale, Arizona. Construction of canals like this one enabled towns and communities to flourish in the Arizona desert.

The community featured golf courses, swimming pools, and shopping.

The Central Arizona Project, which began in 1973, carries water from the Colorado River to Arizona's thirsty desert. It was the largest aqueduct project in history. The project took billions of dollars and nearly 20 years to complete.

Today, Arizona has become increasingly diverse. In 1999, women held all five of the state's top jobs. In 2010, the state passed the country's toughest *immigration* law. The contro-

A crowd of people demonstrates in Phoenix against Arizona's strict anti-illegal immigration law, which passed in 2010. Some elements of the law were struck down in 2012 by the U.S. Supreme Court in the case Arizona v. United States. However, the provision that allows police officers to detain a person in order to investigate his or her immigration status was retained in the legislation.

versial legislation allows police to check the status of people they believe to be in the country illegally.

Government

Arizonans finalized their constitution on December 12, 1911. Arizona became a state three months later. The state still operates under its original constitution, although it has been amended several times.

Arizona's state legislature has two bodies: the Senate and House of Representatives. Arizona has 30 legislative districts, and each district elects one state senator and two repre-

sentatives. All legislators serve two-year terms, and can serve a maximum of four terms in a row. After a two-year period out of office, legislators may serve again.

Governors can serve up to two, four-year terms consecutively. That same governor can serve again, but only after retiring from office for four years.

Arizona's judicial branch includes a five-member Supreme Court, as well as several lower courts. Supreme Court justices serve for six years.

With the 16th-largest population in the nation as of 2014, Arizona wields

Some Famous Arizonans

Labor organizer César Chávez (1927–1993) was born in Yuma. He founded what became the United Farm Workers and later led the Delano grape strike in 1965.

Apache leader Geronimo (ca. 1829–1909) fought against Mexico and the United States to protect the Apache way of life.

Two Republican presidential candidates have called Arizona home: Barry Goldwater (1909–1998) faced off against Lyndon B. Johnson in 1964. Goldwater, a businessman, represented Arizona in the U.S. Senate for 30 years. John McCain (b. 1936), ran against Barack Obama in 2008. McCain, a veteran of the Vietnam War, represented Arizona in the U.S. House of Representatives from 1983 to 1987, and has represented the state in the U.S. Senate since 1987, when he was elected to replace Goldwater.

U.S. Senator John McCain

Born in Nogales, Charles Mingus (1922–1979) became a jazz bassist and composer.

Sandra Day O'Connor (b. 1930) became the first woman U.S. Supreme Court Justice in 1981. Though born in Texas, she spent childhood summers on her parents' Arizona cattle ranch and served in the state's government before being appointed to the Court by Ronald Reagan.

Sandra Day O'Connor

At age 17, singer Jordin Sparks (b. 1989) became the youngest person to ever win *American Idol*.

Author Stephenie Meyer (b. 1973), who penned the Twilight series of books, lives in Phoenix.

Tuscon's Kerri Strug (b. 1977) competed on the U.S. Gymnastics team in the 1992 and 1996 Olympic Games. Despite an injury, she helped her team earn the gold medal in 1996.

Stephenie Meyer

considerable power in the U.S. federal government. Like all states, Arizona has two U.S. senators. In addition, the state has nine representatives in the U.S. House of Representatives.

Arizona holds 11 electoral votes in U.S. Presidential elections. It is the second fastest-growing state in terms of population, and its 11th electoral vote was added following the 2010 Census.

The Economy

Arizona's economy was $280 billion in 2013, making it the 21st largest state economy in the nation.

Farming plays a major role in Arizona's economy. The state is the fifth-largest U.S. producer of fruits and vegetables including cabbage, citrus fruit, chili peppers, corn, broccoli, cauliflower, melons, lettuce, and spinach. Hay and cotton are important nonfood crops. Arizona ranchers today raise horses, donkeys, and cows.

Copper reigns as king among Arizona's natural resources. The state's mines produce 65 percent of all U.S. copper. Most of the state's miner-

Aerial view of an open pit copper mine near Green Valley. Each year, mines in Arizona produce more than $5 billion worth of copper.

al resources are located in the southern part of the state. They include *deposits* of gold and silver, as well as lead and zinc. Further north lie rich uranium deposits.

In 2013, 39 million people visited Arizona, making tourism one of the largest industries. According to the Arizona Office of Tourism, the travel business contributes almost $20 billion to the state's economy. It also provides jobs for 164,000 Arizonans. One of the biggest attractions is the Grand Canyon, which draws more than 4.3 million visitors each year.

Intel's computer-chip manufacturing facility in Chandler opened in 2013.

Manufacturing is another major component of Arizona's economy. In 2014, *semiconductor* chip maker Intel and aerospace giant Honeywell together employed more than 21,000 Arizonans.

Just like its neighbors in the west, the biggest share of Arizona's economy is in real estate, insurance, and finance at 21 percent. Government is another major player at 14 percent.

About 2.8 million Arizonans held jobs in July 2014. The state's unemployment rate stood at about 7 percent during the same period.

The People

Arizona is a land where cultures come together. The state's population has grown rapidly over the past 55 years, from about 1.3 million people in 1960 to more than 6.7 million today. In recent years, much of that growth has been among Hispanics. According to the U.S. Census Bureau, Hispanics or Latinos made up 30 percent of Arizona's population. Many of them were born in other countries. Whites make up 58 percent of the population.

Native Americans make up about 4.6 percent of Arizona's population, according to the U.S. Census Bureau. That's much higher than the U.S. average of 1.2 percent. In fact, Arizona is home to 22 Native American tribes today. Phoenix has the third-largest population of Native Americans in the nation.

Compared to national averages, Arizonans have slightly lower levels of education and higher poverty levels. While about the same number of people graduate from high school compared to the U.S. as a whole (85 percent), fewer graduate from a four-year college (27 percent). Almost 17 percent of Arizonans are very poor.

Major cities

With more than 300 days of sunshine each year, *Phoenix* is aptly called "The Valley of the Sun." The city is the sixth largest in the U.S. with a population of about 1.5 million. The city grew up around the site of former Hohokam irrigation canals. In the 1860s, Jack Swilling improved the canals to bring water to valley farmers, who grew food for soldiers at nearby Camp McDowell. Phoenix became a city in 1881.

Today the military, high-tech workers, and retirees call Phoenix home. Arizona State University also is located there, and the city serves as the

Over the past 40 years, Phoenix has grown rapidly, and currently ranks as the sixth largest city by population in the U.S. It also has the distinction of being the most populous state capital.

Modern skyscrapers rise behind colorful 19th-century buildings in downtown Tuscon.

capital of Arizona.

Most of Arizona's largest cities are part of the greater Phoenix area, including **Chandler, Glendale, Gilbert, Mesa, Peoria, Scottsdale, Surprise,** and **Tempe.** Along with Phoenix, these cities are home to more than 4.2 million people, making the Phoenix area the 14th largest metro area in the United States.

To the southeast, **Tucson** is Arizona's second largest city with a population of 520,000. The Spanish established a presidio, or fort, at Tucson in 1775 to fight the Apache. Once Arizona became a U.S. territory, Tucson served as the territorial capital from 1867 to 1877. Today, Tucson is home to several military installations and the University of Arizona, which serve as the area's major employers.

The site of present day **Yuma** (population 196,000) was a popular place to cross the Colorado River from Arizona into California. During the Gold Rush of 1849, 60,000 miners trudged through on their way to California. In 1877, the Southern Pacific railroad carried people between Yuma and California. Today two military installations and farming serve as the cornerstones of the city's economy. Yuma serves as the Yuma County seat.

Prescott (population 40,000) was the original capital of the Arizona Territory. It was home to the government from 1864 to 1867, when the capital was moved to Tucson. Prescott served as the capital a second time from 1877 until 1889.

Further Reading

Derzipilski, Kathleen and Amanda Hudon. *Arizona. It's My State*. New York: Marshall Cavendish Benchmark, 2012.

Frisch, Nate. *Grand Canyon National Park*. Mankato, Minn.: Creative Education, 2014.

Spilsbury, Richard. *Geronimo. Hero Journal*. Mankato, Minn.:Heinemann-Raintree, 2013.

Internet Resources

http://azgovernor.gov/AZSpotlight/Kids_Main.asp

The governor's office maintains the Arizona Kids Page with information about the state's government, wildlife, history, and more.

http://www.loc.gov/teachers/classroommaterials/primarysourcesets/states/arizona/

The Library of Congress has several primary resources to explore, including photographs, digitized bills, and an audio recording of the state's song.

http://www.visitarizona.com/

Arizona's Office of Tourism explores the Grand Canyon State region by region.

 # Text-Dependent Questions

1. Which river forms Arizona's western border?
2. Why did cotton become an important crop in Arizona?
3. How many towns have served as Arizona's state capital?

 # Research Project

Select one of Arizona's original Native American tribes, for example Pueblo or Hohokam. Using your library and internet resources, research the group's culture, including how it lived and worked, and its religious beliefs. Write a two-page overview of your findings.

CALIFORNIA REPUBLIC

 ## California at a Glance

Area: 163,695 sq mi (423,968 sq km)[1].
  3rd largest state
  Land: 155,779 sq mi (403,465 sq km)
  Water: 7,915 sq mi (20,500 sq km)
Highest elevation: Mt. Whitney,
  14,494 feet (4,418 m)
Lowest elevation: Death Valley, 282
  feet (86 m) below sea level

Statehood: September 9,1850
  (31st state)

Capital: Sacramento

Population: 38,802,500
  (largest state)[2]

State nickname: Golden State
State bird: California quail
State flower: golden poppy

[1] U.S. Census Bureau
[2] U.S. Census Bureau, 2014 estimate

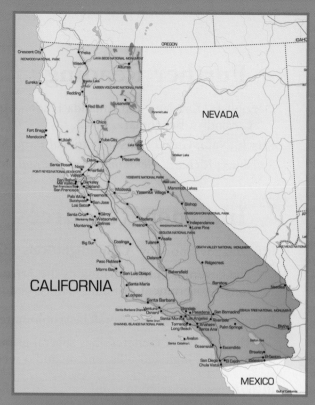

California

California's state seal perfectly sums up the Golden State. The Roman goddess Minerva stands for wisdom and trade. She is an apt symbol, as California has the largest economy in the nation. The seal also shows California's rich resources, including mining and farming.

Geography

California is the third largest U.S. state in area, bigger even than many countries. In all, the Golden State covers 163,695 square miles (423,968 square kilometers).

The Pacific Ocean serves as California's western border. To the south lies Mexico. Oregon makes up the state's northern border, while Nevada and Arizona lie to the east. California also includes many islands, like the eight Channel Islands in southern California and the Farallon Islands off San Francisco.

Mountain ranges are one of the most defining features of the California landscape. The Coast Ranges run along the Pacific, while the Sierra Nevada parallel them inland. At 14,494 feet (4,418 m) above sea level, the Sierra Nevada's Mt. Whitney is the highest point in the continental U.S. To the north, portions of the

Cascades and Klamath Mountains swoop down into the state.

Sandwiched between the mountain ranges lies the Central Valley, the food basket of the U.S. Dotted with farms, this area stretches more than 20,000 square miles (51,800 sq km). More than 230 different crops are grown in the Central Valley.

To the southeast lies the Mojave Desert, the largest in the state. The Mojave also boasts the lowest point in the entire U.S., Death Valley at 282 feet (86 m) below sea level.

The Sacramento and San Joaquin Rivers begin at the Sierra Nevada. Melting snow fills the rivers each spring. The Coast Ranges feed smaller rivers like the Salina, Klamath, and Russian Rivers. Manmade canals carry water from peaks in the north to the parched south.

California's largest lake is the Salton Sea in southern California,

 Words to Understand in This Chapter

appeal—ask to reconsider.

boycott—a protest that includes refusing to do or buy something.

Catholicism—the faith of the Roman Catholic Church.

colonist—a person who settles a new area.

compromise—an agreement between two groups that involves both sides giving up some demands.

internment—temporarily put in prison during wartime.

mission—a settlement formed to spread religious ideas.

naturalized—a legal citizen of a country where one was not born.

rancho—a ranch.

riot—a noisy or violent public disturbance.

Malibu is one of southern California's many popular beaches. Pictured here are the cliffs at Point Dume.

Father and son pause to admire the giant Sequoia (Redwood) trees in the Muir Woods, one of the few remaining Redwood groves near San Francisco.

Zabriskie Point is located in Death Valley National Park.

Yosemite Valley is the most popular attraction in Yosemite National Park, visited by more than 3.5 million people each year. The entire park covers an area of 1,169 square miles (3,028 sq km) on the eastern side of central California.

Few dinosaur fossils are found in California, because the state was under water for much of the Mesozoic era. However, the state is home to the La Brea Tar Pits in Los Angeles, where fossils of Ice Age mammals like saber-toothed cats and mammoths have been found preserved in natural asphalt. This mammoth sculpture is located outside the George C. Page Museum, where many of the fossils found in the tar pits are displayed.

measuring 45 miles by 20 miles (72 km to 32 km). The lake formed in 1905 when the Colorado River flooded, breaking gates that kept the river contained.

California's weather draws many people to the state. Beach temperatures average in the 60s and 70s (16° to 24°C) in the summer with lows in the 40s and 50s (4° to 10°C) in winter. The deserts get much hotter, topping 100°F (38°C) in the summer. In winter, temperatures in the mountains fall below freezing. These areas get plentiful snow, receiving up to 100 inches (254 cm) of precipitation annually.

History

California's history stretches back at least 14,000 years when the first people arrived. By the 1500s, at least 300,000 Native Americans lived in the area. They hailed from 60 different groups speaking 90 different languages.

Most of the early people hunted small game and gathered food. Others fished. A few farmed to support their own families. Many relied upon acorns, which they gathered and ground into meal for porridge.

The Spanish began their exploration and conquest of American lands in the early 1500s. In 1542, Spanish leaders sent a sea captain, Juan Rodríguez Cabrillo, north from Mexico. His goal was to explore the California coast and find a route to the Atlantic Ocean. On September 28, he entered San Diego Bay. He was the first white man to see what is now California. Other Europeans followed. Sir Francis Drake explored the San Francisco Bay Area in 1579, claiming the area for England. Over the next century, however, Europeans left

California Attractions

One of the most-recognized bridges in the world, San Francisco's Golden Gate Bridge attracts more than 10 million people a year. They walk, drive, and bike across its span.

From refreshing waterfalls and sharp cliffs to towering sequoias, Yosemite National Park's glacier-carved landscape lies east of San Francisco.

The Disneyland theme park in Anaheim opened its doors in 1955. Today the resort draws 14 million visitors a year and includes a themed shopping area and several hotels.

From Mann's Chinese Theater and the Hollywood Walk of Fame to studio tours, the glitz and glamour of Hollywood brings people from around the world.

Founded in 1916, the San Diego Zoo today covers 100 acres (41 ha). Caesar, a kodiak bear, was the first animal to make his home at the zoo, but today more than 3,700 animals live there.

The church at San Juan Bautista, built in 1797, was one of the 21 Spanish missions established in Alta California between 1769 and 1823.

California largely unsettled.

By 1769, the Spanish government feared they would lose control of the area if *colonists* did not settle there. Father Junípero Serra, along with military leader José de Gálvez and Captain Gaspar de Portolá, embarked on a "Sacred Expedition" to settle the area. Serra, a Franciscan monk, set up the first *mission* in what is now San Diego. At the time, California was part of the Spanish colony in the new world known as New Spain.

Eventually 21 missions sprouted up along California's coast. The purpose of these missions was to spread **Catholicism** to the native peoples. The Spanish forced Native Americans to leave their lands and work at the missions. The natives built the missions, farmed, raised animals, cooked, sewed, and learned trades. They learned Spanish and attended church.

Yet, the native people had their own beliefs and ways of life. Many rebelled. In 1775, natives burned the San Diego mission, killing a priest and two others. Despite unrest, the mission system continued for 60 more years.

In 1821, the New Spain colony gained its independence from Spain as the nation of Mexico. Three years later, Alta California, as it was called, became a Mexican territory. The Mexican government began closing missions in 1833. It turned over some of the lands to the mission Indians who had worked them. The Mexican government encouraged its people to settle in California by granting pieces of land, called *ranchos*.

During the 1840s, settlers from the

east arrived in California. Fur trappers came to trap beaver as early as 1826. In 1841, the first wagon trains began to arrive, carrying European settlers with dreams of a better life. To reach California, the wagon trains had to navigate treacherous passes through the Sierra Nevada range.

Some never made it, though. In 1846, a group of pioneers known as the Donner Party became trapped in the snowy mountains. Many people died—those who survived ate dogs, leather, and possibly the dead bodies of their traveling companions before they were rescued in March 1847.

The year 1846 also marked the beginning of a U.S. war against Mexico. Before Californians knew the war had begun, a small band of non-Mexican settlers staged a revolt. The Mexican governor had threatened to take away land from non-Mexicans living in California. U.S. Army Captain John Frémont encouraged settlers around Sonoma to rebel. They succeeded and formed the Republic of California. The Republic's new flag leant its name to the revolt: the Bear Flag Revolt. The new Republic did not last long. Three weeks later the Republic pledged allegiance to the United States.

The Bear Flag Monument in Sonoma commemorates the revolt of California settlers against Mexican rule that began in June 1846.

A miner's camp in California during the first year of the Gold Rush.

In 1848, the U.S. war with Mexico ended, and California officially became a U.S. territory. In 1849, delegates met in Monterey to draft a territorial constitution, which outlawed slavery. The U.S. Congress did not immediately agree to make California a state. Admitting California as a free state would upset the balance of free and slave states—an important political consideration at the time. Finally, a *compromise* admitted California as a free state and organized Utah and Nevada as U.S. territories. The same bill strengthened fugitive slave laws. California joined the United States on September 9, 1850.

Around the time of statehood, California's population skyrocketed. On January 24, 1848, a man named James Marshall discovered gold at Sutter's mill in Sacramento, sparking a

Gold Rush. Almost overnight, California's population grew from 10,000 to over 100,000. Many of these settlers were foreign born—not only from Europe, but also from Asia, particularly China.

After the Gold Rush ended, many Chinese stayed in California. Others came in the decades that followed. More than 10,000 Chinese immigrant laborers helped to build the Central Pacific Railroad. That project broke ground in Sacramento in 1863, and tracks were laid east through California, over the Sierra Nevada range, and into Utah.

On May 10, 1869, the Central Pacific tracks were joined to rails being laid by the Union Pacific Railroad, at Promontory Point, Utah. This completed the Transcontinental Railroad, linking the United States from coast to coast. The railroad made westward travel faster and safer, as a person could travel from New York to California in a week or less, as opposed to a trip by ship or wagon that would take many months to complete.

The 20th century brought both booms and busts to California. A thunderous boom awoke San Francisco on the morning of April 18, 1906. That day, a violent earthquake

The Central Pacific needed more than 10,000 workers to lay tracks for the railroad, but had trouble recruiting even 20 percent of that number from miners and settlers in California. Railroad officials solved this problem by hiring Chinese immigrants, including the men on this work crew. Although the Chinese were willing to work hard for little pay, they were not always welcome in California, and often faced racial prejudice and discrimination.

San Franciscans watch as their city burns in the aftermath of a powerful earthquake, 1906. At least 3,000 people were killed in the earthquake and subsequent fires, which were caused by ruptured gas lines and overturned cookstoves that ignited wooden buildings. The fires raged for three days, destroying roughly 25,000 buildings and leaving more than 250,000 people homeless.

destroyed much of the city. Rebuilding took years.

Meanwhile, to the south, the city of Los Angeles blossomed. Although moviemaking did not originate in California, it soon became a favored location for many film directors. In 1913, the newly completed Los Angeles aqueduct carried water from the Owens Valley, fueling the city's growth.

The Great Depression in the 1930s brought a new wave of migration. More than 300,000 people fled from places like Oklahoma and arrived in the Golden State looking for work. Yet there were not enough jobs to go around.

After 1941, the U.S. entry into World War II jump-started the state's economy. Women turned wrenches in aircraft factories. However, for Japanese Americans living in California, World War II brought temporary *internment* at two relocation camps: Manzanar and Tule Lake.

California continued to grow rapidly in the latter half of the 20th century. Sometimes hostilities between different groups boiled over. Racial tensions flared during the Watts *riots* of 1965, and again during the Los

(Left) The day after the Japanese attack on Pearl Harbor in December 1941, the Japanese-American owner of this store in Oakland placed this large sign proclaiming his allegiance. Nonetheless, war hysteria soon led to the internment of many Californians of Japanese descent, including these young women (right) at the Tule Lake camp near the California-Oregon border. Decades later, the U.S. government officially apologized for detaining these U.S. citizens.

During 2000 and 2001, California experienced a serious energy crisis, which resulted in huge increases in electricity prices as well as regular and widespread blackouts. The crisis led to significant changes in the structure and distribution of energy in the state. Today, California is a leading producer of renewable energy, and power produced by wind farms like this one near Tehachapi provided roughly 20 percent of the state's electrical output.

Police and National Guardsmen patrol a burned-out shopping center during the 1992 riots in South Central Los Angeles. During six days of rioting, more than 1,100 buildings—many of them stores owned by Asian Americans—were damaged or destroyed by fire and 53 people were killed.

Angeles riots of 1992. In 1965, friction over conditions for farmworkers grew. Filipino and Latino farm workers, led by César Chávez, organized a *boycott* against grape growers until conditions improved.

The 1960s and 1970s saw the development of California's high-tech industry. Firms like Hewlett-Packard, Bell Laboratories, and Xerox established facilities near San Francisco, in part because of this area's proximity to Stanford University and other major research insititutions.

In 1976, Steve Wozniak and Steve Jobs sold their first Apple computer, which had been built in a garage. The computing industry flourishes today in this area, which is often referred to as Silicon Valley.

Government

In 1849, California adopted its first state constitution. Today, the state operates under a revised constitution that was adopted in 1879. This constitution has been amended 521 times, and is the third-longest constitution in the world.

Jerry Brown is the longest-serving governor in California's history. He served in that position from 1975 to 1983, and was re-elected as governor in 2011.

California has a bicameral legislature. The State Senate consists of 40 senators who serve four-year terms. Terms are staggered so half of the senate is elected every two years. The State Assembly has 80 members who serve two-year terms. Legislators may serve no more than 12 years total during their lifetime.

Among the states, California is unusual in that it has a process by which members of the public can propose laws or amendments to the state constitution, and the voters can decide whether they should be approved through elections. These are called "ballot propositions." In recent years, some ballot propositions have been very controversial.

California's governor is elected to a four-year term in office, and can serve no more than two terms. The judicial branch includes the Supreme Court, courts of *appeal*, and county superior courts. Californians elect their judges.

As the most populous state, California has an important role in national affairs. California has 53 legislators in the U.S. House of

California's State Capitol building in Sacramento, completed in 1874, houses the State Assembly as well as the office of the governor.

U.S. Congresswoman Nancy Pelosi, shown here riding in a San Francisco parade, is an important leader of the national Democratic Party. She has served in Congress since 1987. From 2007 to 2011, she was Speaker of the U.S. House of Representatives, making her the highest-ranking female politician in U.S. history.

California is an important producer of agricultural products. (Left) The sun sets over a vineyard in the Napa Valley, which is internationally known for its wine production. (Right) A farmer sprays rows of strawberries in Orange County.

Representatives, the most of any state. Like all U.S. states, it is represented by two senators in Congress.

For U.S. presidential elections, California hold 55 electoral votes. A candidate needs 270 electoral votes to win, so winning California will get the candidate 20 percent of required total.

The Economy

At about $2 trillion per year, California's economy is the biggest in the nation. In fact, if California was an independent country it would have the ninth-largest economy in the world, right behind Brazil and the United Kingdom, and ahead of countries like Italy, Mexico, and Spain.

California is the biggest agricultural producer in the country. Major crops include grapes, almonds, rice, fruits, and vegetables, along with hay and grass. Cotton, first grown in the 1920s, remains an important crop today.

Spanish settlers first brought cows to the state in the 1500s. Today California is the largest producer of milk in the country. It ranks fourth among beef-producing states.

The state is rich in natural resources. Even though the Gold Rush is long over, the Golden State remains the nation's fifth-biggest supplier of minerals. In 2013, only two other states produced more crude oil than California: Texas and Alaska. California's prime location on the Pacific has created the nation's fourth-largest fishing industry. Finally, the state's vast forests rank it among the top three states in timber production.

California has a large computer and electronics manufacturing industry based in Silicon Valley. Companies like Apple, Google, and Facebook have their headquarters there.

In 2014, 17 million Californians held jobs. Historically, California's unemployment rate has been higher than the national average. In July 2014, it stood at 7.4%.

The People

California's unique history and large population have created a state with a diverse culture. One out of every eight Americans lives in the Golden State. According to the U.S. Census Bureau,

Silicon Valley, to the south of the San Francisco Bay, is home to many of the world's largest technology corporations, including Oracle (in Redwood City), Hewlett-Packard (in Palo Alto), and Google (in Mountain View).

Famous People from California

Two 20th century U.S. Presidents hailed from California. Richard Nixon (1913–1994) was born and raised in Yorba Linda. Though born in Illinois, Ronald Reagan (1911–2004), who also served as California's governor, spent much of his life in Los Angeles and at his ranch near Santa Barbara.

Richard M. Nixon   Ronald Reagan

Many famous writers have called California home. Poet Robert Frost (1874–1963) and author Jack London (1876–1916) were born in San Francisco. Nobel-Prize winner John Steinbeck (1902–1968) hailed from Salinas and famously wrote about the state in *Tortilla Flats*, *East of Eden*, and *In Dubious Battle*.

Sisters and tennis pros Venus (b. 1980) and Serena Williams (b. 1981) grew up in Compton where they trained on the public tennis courts. Golf great Tiger Woods (b. 1975) was born in Cypress, while NASCAR driver Jeff Gordon (b. 1971) grew up in Vallejo. Snowboarder Shaun White (b. 1986), who won gold medals in the 2006 and 2010 Winter Olympics, was born in San Diego.

Dr. Sally Ride (1951–2012), the first U.S. woman in space, was a native of Los Angeles. So was Ellen Ochoa (b. 1958), the first Hispanic woman in space.

Earl Warren (1891–1974) was Chief Justice of the United States Supreme Court from 1953 to 1969. During that time the Court made many rulings that had a great effect on American life, including the *Brown vs. The Board of Education* decision in 1954, which declared segregation in public schools unconstitutional.

Steve Jobs

Apple Computer co-founders Steve Jobs (1955–2011) and Steve Wozniak (b. 1950) both grew up in California.

Many stars make their home in California. However, superstars Angelina Jolie (b. 1975), Cameron Diaz (b. 1972), and Leonardo DiCaprio (b. 1974) are just a few who were born in the state.

Los Angeles is the second-largest city in the United States. The Greater Los Angeles region, which includes the city as well as Orange, San Bernardino, Riverside, Ventura, and Los Angeles counties, is home to more than 18 million people.

the state's population today is more than 38 million.

According to Census Bureau estimates, Hispanic and Latinos became the largest ethnic group in 2014, numbering about 39 percent of the population. This group narrowly surpassed the white population, which was 38.8 percent. This made California only the third state with a non-white plurality. According to the 2010 U.S. Census, other major ethnic groups in California include Asian Americans at 13 percent and African-Americans at almost 6.2 percent.

A quarter of Californians were born in a foreign country. Most immigrants hail from Latin America; how-

Los Angeles Lakers star Kobe Bryant holds up a trophy after winning the 2009 NBA championship. The Lakers are among the most successful NBA franchises, having won 16 titles.

percentage of Californians hold college degrees.

Major Cities

With nearly 4 million people, **Los Angeles** is California's largest city and the second-largest in the U.S. Following the establishment of the Mission San Gabriel, the first four families arrived from Mexico in June 1781 to form a pueblo, or nonreligious settlement.

Today, the "City of Angels" is known as the entertainment capital of the world. Aside from recording studios and movie backlots, L.A. is home to the University of Southern California and the University of

ever, 75 percent are **naturalized** citizens or have legal immigration status. In recent years, more immigrants have come from Asia. Almost half of Californians speak a language other than English at home.

The Census Bureau reports that Californians have slightly lower high school graduation rates than the U.S. average overall. However, a greater

The Hollywood sign has become a landmark representing the film industry in southern California.

California-Los Angeles (UCLA). It also boasts growing fashion, health-care, and technology industries.

San Diego was the first settlement in California. Today, it is the state's second-largest city with 2.3 million residents. The city's beaches sit side-by-side with cultural attractions like Balboa Park. The city is the birthplace of naval aviation and home to several military bases

Founded in 1777, ***San Jose*** also started as a pueblo. The city served as the state capital during California's earliest years. Today, San Jose is a cor-nerstone of Silicon Valley with 6,600

The U.S.-Mexico border crossing station in the San Ysidro neighborhood of San Diego is so busy that in 2011 the U.S. and Mexico began a three-year project to expand the facilities.

San Francisco is known for its hills, as well as for its cable car system of public transportation. In the background of this photo, the notorious prison Alcatraz can be seen in San Francisco Bay.

technology companies providing jobs for 254,000 people. The city's population is about 1.7 million.

Known as the "City by the Bay," **San Francisco** contains a mix of neighborhoods. It boasts a vibrant wharf, one of the largest Chinatowns outside of China, and Haight-Ashbury, home of the original hippies. The population of San Francisco is about 800,000 today.

In 1839, John Sutter began farming in the **Sacramento** area. Discovery of gold at a mill on his property launched the Gold Rush in 1848. In 1854, Sacramento became the state capital. Today, it is home to most state government buildings and has a population of about 470,000.

Fresno is the largest city in California's fertile Central Valley. The city also has a strong military presence thanks to Lemoore Naval Air Station. Fresno has a population of about 500,000.

Further Reading

Brimner, Larry Dane. *Strike!* Honesdale, Penn.: Calkins Creek, 2014.

Duffield, Katy S. *California History for Kids: Missions, Miners, and Moviemakers in the Golden State*. Chicago: Chicago Review Press, 2012.

Hamilton, Sam C. *Discovering Mission San Diego De Alcala*. New York: Cavendish Square Publishing, 2014.

Orr, Tamra B. *California*. New York: Scholastic's Children's Press, 2014.

Internet Resources

http://www.capitolmuseum.ca.gov/

Learn about California or take a virtual Capitol tour on the Capitol Museum site.

http://www.pbs.org/wgbh/amex/goldrush/

Experience California's Gold Rush history on PBS's American Experience site.

http://memory.loc.gov/ammem/cbhtml/cbhome.html

The Library of Congress maintains first-person narratives of California's early days on its "California as I Saw It" site.

 # Text-Dependent Questions

1. Why did the Spanish settle California?
2. Name two important rivers in the state.
3. Name three natural resources. How important are these to California's economy?

 # Research Project

The Gold Rush forever changed the face of California. Use library and internet resources to learn more about the period. Who moved to California during this time? What was life like for these people?

Nevada
at a Glance

Area: 110,572 sq mi (286,380 sq km)[1]. The 7th-largest state
  Land: 109,781 sq mi (284,332 sq km)
  Water: 791 sq mi (2,049 sq km)
Highest elevation: Boundary Peak, 13,140 feet (4,005 m)
Lowest elevation: along the Colorado River, 470 feet (143 m) above sea level

Statehood: Oct. 31, 1864 (36th state)
Capital: Carson City

Population: 2,839,099 (35th largest state)[2]

State nickname: the Silver State
State bird: mountain bluebird
State flower: sagebrush

[1] *U.S. Census Bureau*
[2] *U.S. Census Bureau, 2014 estimate*

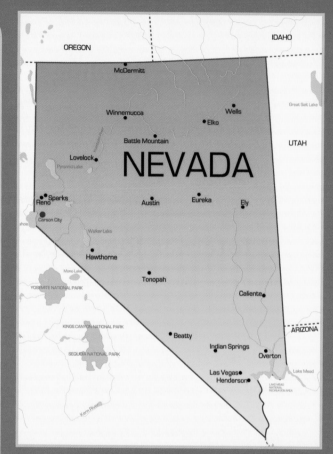

Nevada

Despite its dry weather, Nevada's name means "snow-capped" in Spanish. The state takes its name from the Sierra Nevada, a large mountain range that lies mostly in California. Padre Pedro Font named the mountains in 1776.

Geography

Covering 110,572 square miles (286,380 square kilometers), Nevada is the seventh-largest state by area. Five states encircle Nevada. California forms the entire western border. To the north lie Oregon and Idaho. To the east sit Utah and Arizona.

The Great *Basin* covers much of Nevada. It includes short mountain ranges interspersed with depressions called basins. Nevada's mountain ranges typically measure between 7,000 and 10,000 feet (2,100 and 3,050 meters) tall. The state's highest point is Boundary Peak, at 13,140 feet (4,005 m), which lies near the California border. The lowest spot sits along the Colorado River in the southeastern portion of the state, measuring 470 feet (143 m) above sea level. Near Las Vegas, the Mojave Desert stretches into California.

Aside from the Colorado, Nevada is home to the Humboldt

River, its longest. The river runs about 310 miles, draining the northern part of the state. To the west are the Carson, Walker, and Truckee Rivers, which run into lakes or *sinks*. Located in the northwest, Pyramid Lake is the Silver State's largest lake at 188 square miles (487 sq km). Nearby sits Lake Tahoe, which Nevada shares with California. On Nevada's border with Arizona, the Hoover Dam forms Lake Mead.

Nevada is the driest state in the U.S., experiencing just 9.5 inches (24 cm) of precipitation each year. In the deserts to the south, summer temper-atures top 100°F (38°C). The Great Basin area is much cooler, with winter temperatures dipping below freezing.

History

Nevada's history stretches back 11,000 years, to a time when people tracked mammoth, camel, bison, and horses in the area. Archaeologists have discovered milling stones and evidence of farming in the years before 500 CE. For unknown reasons, early native cultures disappeared. At that time, the ancestors of the Great Basin groups moved into the area, including ancestors of the Shoshone

 # Words to Understand in This Chapter

basin—a bowl-shaped landform.
exchange—to trade one thing for another.
irrigation—to provide water by artificial means.
Mormon—member of the Church of Jesus Christ of Latter Day Saints.
nuclear weapons—a weapon that derives its destructive force from a nuclear reaction, in which many atomic particles collide to produce an enormous amount of energy.
sink—a low area.

Red Rock Canyon is located in the Mojave Desert of southern Nevada. In 1990 it was designated as a National Conservation Area.

A natural arch of red sandstone sits in the Valley of Fire. The stone forma-tions were produced by faulting and erosion over 150 million years. The original Native Americans that lived in the Nevada region carved petroglyphs into some of the rocks some 3,000 years ago.

Nevada Attractions

There's far more to Las Vegas than gambling at casinos. Las Vegas is a top destination for concerts and performances. Casinos also feature shopping, swimming, and dining.

Built during the Great Depression, the Hoover Dam is a National Historic Landmark. Today, the dam generates electricity for 1.3 million people in the western states. Tours include a 70-second elevator trip to the bottom of Black Canyon.

In the winter months, visitors can swoosh down the slopes at Lake Tahoe's ski resorts. During the summer, people enjoy hiking, swimming, and boating.

At Great Basin National Park tourists visit the Lehman caves, catch a fish, or enjoy hiking among the ancient bristlecone pine trees.

Known as one of America's top 5 car museums, the National Automobile Museum in Reno boasts a collection of more than 200 cars. Opened in 1989, the museum grew from the collection of Bill Harrah, founder of Harrah's Casino and Resorts.

Skiing at Lake Tahoe.

Hoover Dam and an adjacent highway bridge.

and Northern and Southern Paiute. The Washo also made their home in Nevada.

Few European settlers ventured into Nevada before the 1800s. The first European may have been the priest Francisco Garcés in 1776. He followed the Colorado River from modern day Mexico before heading west to California.

Fur trappers marked the next wave of European travelers. In 1826, Peter Skene Ogden and Jedediah Strong Smith explored the state independently of each other. Both sought to trap beavers, intending to *exchange* their fur for money.

In 1843–1844, John Frémont began a more systematic exploration of Nevada. He discovered Pyramid Lake on his first journey and found a pass through the Sierra Nevada to California. In 1845, he explored the Great Basin region, which he named.

Though the Spanish never settled present-day Nevada, they claimed this region. When Mexico won its independence from Spain in 1821, the area became part of Mexico. Finally,

During 1843–44, John C. Frémont, nicknamed "The Pathfinder," explored Oregon, Nevada, and California. He played an key role in the revolt of California against Mexican rule, was a presidential candidate in 1856, and was later appointed governor of the Arizona Territory.

after the U.S. won its war against Mexico in 1848, Nevada became part of the United States. By 1850, the U.S. government had divided the former Mexican lands into three parts: the Utah Territory, which included Nevada; the Arizona Territory; and California, which was admitted as a state.

 Did You Know?

Great Basin bristlecone pines, found in Nevada, are the oldest living tree. The oldest pine, called Prometheus, was 4,900 years old when it was cut down in 1964.

(Left) Virginia City, as it appeared in 1867. By that time, the boom town had a population of nearly 25,000. (Right) Miners wheel carts filled with ore out of a shaft at the Comstock Lode, the first major silver mine in the United States.

Meanwhile, during the late 1840s, the California Gold Rush brought scores of wagon trains from the eastern U.S. through the Silver State. Few of these people stayed, however, until the **Mormons** arrived. This religious group sent missionaries from Utah to the Lake Tahoe and Las Vegas areas. They established Mormon Station (now Genoa) near Lake Tahoe in 1851. It was the first white settlement in the state. Soon after, the discovery of gold in nearby Gold Canyon began to draw hundreds of hopeful miners.

In 1859, the discovery of the Comstock Lode gave miners yet another reason to call Nevada home. The area was rich in gold and silver. Seemingly overnight a whole town

 Did You Know?

Samuel Clemens, better known as Mark Twain, journeyed to Nevada in 1861. He recorded his observations of life in the territory in a book called *Roughing It.*

sprang up, made of tents, barrels, mud, and anything else men could find. This "boom town" became known as Virginia City, and soon had a population of more than 20,000.

The newcomers in Nevada refused to acknowledge the Utah territorial government. Instead they petitioned for Nevada to become a separate territory. In 1861, President James Buchanan granted Nevada's request.

As miners flocked to Nevada, tensions with the native people grew. Conflict broke out during the Battle of Pyramid Lake in 1860. A settler kidnapped two Indian women, sparking bloodshed on both sides. The fighting ended quickly, but the ill will persisted for months.

During the Civil War, President Abraham Lincoln admitted Nevada as a free state. It officially joined the U.S. on October 31, 1864. By 1867, the state had added two sections of territory to the east and south, establishing the current borders.

The construction of railroads spurred more growth. Finished in 1869, the Transcontinental Railroad

Smelting works like this one at Oreana were needed to produce pure silver from mined rock, called ore. The process involved heating the ore so that the silver melted and could be extracted.

marched through the state. Towns like Reno sprouted along the rail lines.

As silver production increased in the 1870s, prices fell. At the same time, the U.S. government stopped making silver dollars. The state sank into a 20-year economic depression. A second mining boom lifted Nevada's economy in 1900.

Meanwhile, *irrigation* projects strengthened agriculture in the state after a drought throughout the 1880s and 1890s took its toll on hay farming and cattle raising. Started in 1902, the

This photo from 1910 shows men gambling on roulette at a Reno saloon. Although a 1909 law made gambling illegal in Nevada, over time the rules were relaxed to allow certain games. In 1931, a new law was passed permitting open gambling in the state.

Newlands Project authorized dams and canals allowing farmers to transform 87,500 acres (35,410 ha) of desert in western Nevada into fertile farmland. During the 1920s, talks began for an even larger water project —the Hoover Dam on the Colorado River near Las Vegas. Construction began in 1931, just as the U.S. economy was sinking into the Great Depression. The project provided jobs for thousands of people during a difficult time. The dam was completed in 1935.

Two other things spurred Nevada's economic development during the 20th century: quick divorces and legalized gambling. In most states, obtaining a divorce was a long and difficult process. In Reno, judges granted divorces easily to residents who had lived in Nevada for as little as six months. By 1931, the waiting time was reduced to six weeks, and Reno became known as the "divorce capital of the world."

Gambling had been a way of life in many mining towns. When Nevada became a territory in 1861, the legislature outlawed the activity. For decades, Nevada alternated between legalizing and outlawing gambling. All the while the games of chance continued. Eventually, the state government

The Hoover Dam on the Colorado River created Lake Mead, the largest reservoir in the United States. When the lake is full, it is 112 miles (180 km) long and covers 247 square miles (398 sq km). Lake Mead is around 500 feet (152 m) deep at its greatest depth. Many Nevadans, as well as tourists, visit the lake for boating and recreation.

legalized gambling and imposed taxes on the proceeds. During the 1940s and 1950s, this spurred the growth of resorts in places like Las Vegas and Reno.

The Cold War brought a new industry to the state. In 1950, the U.S. government began to test *nuclear weapons* at the Nevada Test Site, 65 miles (105 km) from Las Vegas. The site drew engineers and researchers to the area, many of whom commuted from Las Vegas. Testing moved underground in 1961. There it continued until the program ended in 1992, when President George H.W. Bush announced a ban on nuclear weapons testing. The National Cancer Institute has traced thousands of cases of thyroid cancer to the 1950s testing program.

Beginning in the 1950s, nuclear weapons were detonated at the Nevada Test Site.

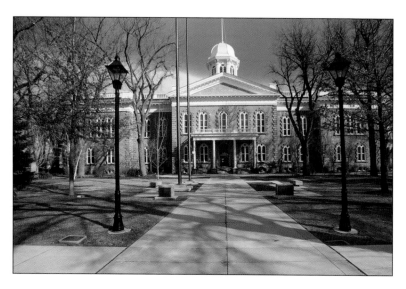

The historic Nevada State Capitol building is located in the capital, Carson City. The structure was completed in 1871, and housed all three branches of the new state's government. Nevada's legislature met in the Capitol building for a century, until a new legislative building was constructed in 1971. The state Supreme Court also moved to a new building, in 1937. Today the state governor maintains his office in the Capitol building, which also features exhibits on state history.

The issue of radioactive materials remains controversial in Nevada. After decades of planning, in 2002 the federal government selected Yucca Mountain, 100 miles (161 km) from Las Vegas, as an underground site where spent nuclear fuel and radioactive waste from American power plants could be permanently stored. However, many Nevadans protested against this plan, and it was delayed for many years. President Barack Obama's administration decided in 2010 that Yucca Mountain would not be used for the purpose of storing radioactive waste. As of 2015, a new site for this purpose has not yet been identified.

Government

Nevadans approved their state constitution on September 7, 1864. On October 31 of that year, Nevada became the 36th state. Its constitution remains the basis of the state government today.

Nevada's legislature consists of two houses, the Senate and the Assembly. The number of legislators changes with each U.S. Census. Following the

2010 Census, the legislature included 21 senators and 42 assembly members. Members of the Assembly serve two-year terms, while senators serve for four years. Nevada enacted term limits in 1996, so legislators can serve no more than 12 years in each body.

The governor of Nevada serves a term of four years, with a two-term limit. The judicial branch includes a supreme court of at least three justices, nine district courts, and several courts of appeal.

Because of its small population, Nevada's representation in the federal government is small. Like all states, Nevada has two U.S. Senators; however, the state has just four representatives in the House. However, it's worth noting that due to the state's population growth, Nevada's representation in congress has doubled over the past 30 years. Nevada casts six electoral votes during presidential elections.

Harry Reid has represented Nevada in the U.S. Senate since 1987. From 2007 until 2015, he served as the Senate Majority Leader.

The Economy

In 2015, Nevada ranked 33rd among the states with an economy valued at about $130 billion. Like neighboring California, much of Nevada's economy is based upon services, such as real estate, banking, and insurance. They make up almost 20 percent of the state's gross domestic product.

The state's second-largest industry is tourism, representing 17 percent of the economy. About 52 million tourists visit Nevada annually, bringing in about $20 billion.

For many years, the Silver State has struck it rich with precious metals. The United States is the world's third-largest gold producer, and more than 75 percent of this gold comes from Nevada. The state also produces nearly 40 percent of the nation's silver.

Other valuable metals and minerals are produced from the state's mines as well.

In the late 1800s, Nevada was home to more cows than people. Today, ranchers raise sheep and goats as well as cattle. Nevada farmers grow hay and devote many acres to potatoes. Overall, however, agriculture is a relatively small part of Nevada's economy.

About 1.3 million Nevadans hold jobs. Restaurants and hotels are the

Roughly 37 million people visit Las Vegas each year.

biggest employers, providing around 300,000 jobs. However, the state does not have enough jobs for working-age people. In 2014, Nevada had one of the highest unemployment rates in the nation, at 7.7 percent.

The People

Nevada's population has grown rapidly in recent years. From 2000 to 2010, the state's population grew by 35 percent—the fastest in the nation. According to the U.S. Census Bureau, more than 2.8 million people call the Silver State home, making it the 35th most populous state in the nation.

The 2010 Census showed that whites comprised 54.1 percent of Nevadans, while those identified as Hispanic or Latino comprised 26.5 percent. African-Americans made up almost 7.7 percent of the population.

 ## Some Famous Nevadans

Tennis great Andre Agassi (b. 1970) was born in Las Vegas, as were NASCAR drivers and brothers, Kurt (b. 1978) and Kyle Busch (b. 1985), and major league baseball outfielder Bryce Harper (b. 1992).

Las Vegas is home to entertainers like pianist Liberace (1919–1987), and singer Wayne "Mr. Las Vegas" Newton (b. 1942).

James E. Casey (1888–1983), from small-town Candelaria, founded corporate giant United Parcel Service (UPS).

Comedian Jimmy Kimmel (b. 1967) was raised in Las Vegas.

Pat Nixon (1912–1993), wife of former U.S. President Richard Nixon, was born in Ely.

Prominent Native Americans include Sarah Winnemucca (1844–1891), a Paiute peacemaker who worked as an advocate and educator, and Dat So La Lee (c1829–1925), a famed basket weaver.

Wayne Newton

Reno, nicknamed "The Biggest Little City in the World," is located at the foot of the Sierra Nevada mountain range. Like Las Vegas, it is popular with tourists due to its casinos and entertainment venues, as well as its proximity to the resorts at Lake Tahoe.

Asians made up 7.1 percent, a figure slightly higher than the national average of 5.3 percent.

Nevada's population is quite mobile. More than three-fourths of Nevada's residents were born outside the state, and almost 20 percent were born in another country. About 30 percent of residents speak a language other than English at home.

Nevadans have slightly lower levels of education than the U.S average. While almost a third of all Americans hold college degrees, only 22 percent of Nevada residents in 2012 held at least a bachelor's degree.

Major cities

Known as "Sin City," **Las Vegas** (population 584,044) features casinos with gambling, restaurants, shopping, and world-class entertainment. A French immigrant founded the area's first resort, Twin Lakes, in the 1920s. Visitors could swim, fish, watch movies, ride horses, and play cards for ten cents. The first resorts on the Las Vegas Strip opened their doors in the

1940s and 1950s, setting the tone for Las Vegas's most prominent industry.

Henderson (population 257,729) and *North Las Vegas* (population 216,961) lie just a few miles from Las Vegas. North Las Vegas is home to Nellis Air Force Base, one of the biggest fighter jet bases in the country, as well as the Thunderbird aerobatic team. The Henderson area traces its history to a large magnesium plant built to supply America's military during World War II.

Reno (population 225,221) lies directly on the Central Pacific Railroad, and its location fueled the town's early growth. Gambling and liberal divorce laws turned Reno into Nevada's original "sin city." Today Reno has diversified into other industries like healthcare and high-tech. Along with nearby *Sparks* (population 90,264), Reno also serves as a gateway to the Lake Tahoe recreational area.

Nevada's capital, *Carson City* (population 55,274), was named for Kit Carson. Carson served as John Frémont's scout during his explorations of Nevada during the 1840s. Carson City thrived as a transportation hub during the mining era. The city served as the territorial capital and became the state capital in 1864 when Nevada achieved statehood.

With a population of 18,297, *Elko* is the largest town in the eastern portion of the state. It serves as the county seat for Elko County.

Further Reading

Heinrichs, Ann. *Nevada*. New York: Scholastic's Children's Press, 2014.

Sanford, William R., and Carl R. Green. *John C. Frémont: Courageous Pathfinder in the Wild West*. Berkeley Heights, N.J.: Enslow Publishers, 2013.

Thompson, Linda. *Building the Transcontinental Railroad*. Vero Beach, Fla.: Rourke Educational Media, 2013.

Internet Resources

http://www.clan.lib.nv.us/content.asp?id=1

Nevada Riches: The Land and People of the Silver State provides an interactive overview of Nevada's history.

http://museums.nevadaculture.org/

Nevada's Division of Museums and History oversees a number of museums statewide. The Web site includes a Just for Kids section with information about the Pony Express, wagon trains, and more.

http://www.loc.gov/teachers/classroommaterials/primarysourcesets/states/nevada/

The Library of Congress maintains a number of primary resources pertinent to the history of Nevada, including letters and photographs.

 # Text-Dependent Questions

1. What is Nevada's largest river?
2. Who were the first non-natives to settle Nevada?
3. How big is Nevada's tourism industry?

 # Research Project

Using library and internet resources, research construction of the Hoover Dam. Why was the dam constructed? What was life like for those working on the project? What impact does the dam have today? Write a two-page paper summarizing your findings.

Index

Arizona
    agriculture in, 19
    attractions in, 11
    cities in, 21–22
    climate of, 10, 15
    diversity in, 20
    economy of, 15, 19–20
    facts, 6
    famous people from, 18
    geography of, 7–10
    government of, 17, 19
    history of, 10, 12–17
    nickname of, 6, 7
    population of, 6, 14, 17, 19,
        20–21, 22
    rivers in, 7, 8, *9*, 16
    statehood date, 6

ballot propositions, 37
    See also government
birds, state, 6, 24, 46
Boundary Peak (NV), 46, 47
Buchanan, James, 53
Bush, George H. W., 55

Cabrillo, Juan Rodríguez, 29
California
agriculture in, 38
    attractions in, 29
    cities in, 42–44
    climate in, 28
    diversity in, 41–42
    economy of, 38–39
    facts, 24
    famous people from, 40
    geography of, 25–28
    government of, 36–38
    history of, 28–36
    nickname of, 24
    population of, 24, 33, 39, 41–42

rivers in, 26
    statehood date, 24, 32
Carson, Kit, 13–14, 61
Carson City, NV, 46, *56*, 61
Central Arizona Project, 16
Chávez, César, 18, 36
Clemens, Samuel (Mark Twain), 52
climate, 10, 15, 28, 48
Coronado, Francisco Vázquez de,
    12

Donner Party, 31
Drake, Francis, 29

economy
    of Arizona, 15, 19–20
    of California, 38–39
    of Nevada, 57–59
Elko, NV, 61

Flagstaff, AZ, 10
flowers, state, 6, 24, 46
Font, Pedro, 47
"Four Corners," 7, *9*
Frémont, John, 31, 51, 61
Fresno, CA, 44

Gálvez, José, 30
gambling, 50, 54–55, 60
Garcés, Francisco, 51
geography
    of Arizona, 7–10
    of California, 25–28
    of Nevada, 47–48, *49*
Geronimo, 14, 18
Gold Rush, 12, 22, 32–33, 44, 45,
    52
"Golden State." *See* California
government
    of Arizona, 17, 19

of California, 36–38
    of Nevada, 56–57
Grand Canyon, 7–8, 10, 11, 19
"Grand Canyon State." *See* Arizona

Henderson, NV, 61
Hohokam tribe, 12, 23
Hoover Dam, 50, 54, *55*, 62
Humphrey's Peak (AZ), 6, 8

immigration, 16–17, 33, 41–42
internment camps, 34, *35*

Jobs, Steve, 36, 40
Johnston, Philip, 15

Kino, Eusebio, *12*, 13

Lake Mead, 10, *55*
Lake Tahoe, 48, 50, 52, *60*, 61
Las Vegas, NV, 50, 55, *58*, 60–61
Lincoln, Abraham, 13, 53
Los Angeles, CA, 34, 36, *41*, 42–43

Marshall, James, 32
Mexico, 13, 25, 30, 31–32, 42, *43*,
    51
mining, 13, 14, 19, 52–53, 58
missions, *12*, 13, 30
Mojave Desert, 26, 47, *49*
Mormons, 52
Mt. Whitney (CA), 24, 25

Native American tribes, 12, 13–14,
    20, 23, 28–29, 30, 48, *49*, 53
Navajo tribe, 12, 13–14, 15
Nevada
    agriculture in, 53–54, 58
    attractions in, 50
    cities in, 60–61

Numbers in **bold italics** refer to captions.

climate of, 48
diversity in, 59–60
economy of, 57–59
facts, 46
famous people from, 59
gambling in, 50, 54–55, 60
geography of, 47–48, *49*
government of, 56–57
history of, 48, 51–56
nickname of, 46
nuclear testing in, 55–56
population of, 46, 57, 59–60
rivers in, 47–48
statehood date, 46, 53, 56
Nixon, Richard, 40
Niza, Marco de, 12
North Las Vegas, NV, 61

Ogden, Peter Skene, 51

Phoenix, AZ, 6, 15, 20, 21–22

population
of Arizona, 6, 14, 17, 19, 20–21, 22
of California, 24, 33, 39, 41–42
of Nevada, 46, 57, 59–60
Portolá, Gaspar de, 30
Poston, Charles, 13
Prescott, AZ, 22
Pueblo people, 12, 23

race riots, 34, 36
railroads, 14, 33, 53
Reagan, Ronald, 40
Reid, Harry, **57**
Reno, NV, 50, 53, 54, 55, **60**, 61
Republic of California, 31
See also California
research projects, 23, 45, 62

Sacramento, CA, 24, 32, 33, **37**, 44
San Diego, CA, 30, 43

San Francisco, CA, 29, 33–34, 44
San Jose, CA, 43–44
Serra, Junípero, 30
Silicon Valley, 36, 39, 43–44
"Silver State." *See* Nevada
Smith, Jedediah Strong, 51
Sparks, NV, 61
Swilling, Jack, 21

Taft, William Howard, 14, *15*
Tohono O'odham tribe, 12, 13
tourism, 11, 19, 29, 58, 62
Tucson, AZ, 22

Virginia City, NV, *52*, 53

Webb, Del, 15
Wozniak, Steve, 36, 40

Yuma, AZ, 8, 22

Series Glossary of Key Terms

bicameral—having two legislative chambers (for example, a senate and a house of representatives).

cede—to yield or give up land, usually through a treaty or other formal agreement.

census—an official population count.

constitution—a written document that embodies the rules of a government.

delegation—a group of persons chosen to represent others.

elevation—height above sea level.

legislature—a lawmaking body.

precipitation—rain and snow.

term limit—a legal restriction on how many consecutive terms an office holder may serve.